ALL AROUND THE WORLD
BAHRAIN

by Kristine Spanier, MLIS

pogo

Ideas for Parents and Teachers

Pogo Books let children practice reading informational text while introducing them to nonfiction features such as headings, labels, sidebars, maps, and diagrams, as well as a table of contents, glossary, and index.

Carefully leveled text with a strong photo match offers early fluent readers the support they need to succeed.

Before Reading

- "Walk" through the book and point out the various nonfiction features. Ask the student what purpose each feature serves.
- Look at the glossary together. Read and discuss the words.

Read the Book

- Have the child read the book independently.
- Invite him or her to list questions that arise from reading.

After Reading

- Discuss the child's questions. Talk about how he or she might find answers to those questions.
- Prompt the child to think more. Ask: What did you know about Bahrain before you read this book? What more would you like to learn?

Pogo Books are published by Jump!
5357 Penn Avenue South
Minneapolis, MN 55419
www.jumplibrary.com

Library of Congress Cataloging-in-Publication Data

Names: Spanier, Kristine, author.
Title: Bahrain / by Kristine Spanier.
Description: Minneapolis, MN: Jump!, [2022]
Series: All around the world
Includes index. | Audience: Ages 7-10
Identifiers: LCCN 2020050703 (print)
LCCN 2020050704 (ebook)
ISBN 9781645279976 (hardcover)
ISBN 9781645279983 (paperback)
ISBN 9781645279990 (ebook)
Subjects: LCSH: Bahrain–Juvenile literature.
Classification: LCC DS247.B2 S63 2022 (print)
LCC DS247.B2 (ebook) | DDC 953.65–dc23
LC record available at https://lccn.loc.gov/2020050703
LC ebook record available at https://lccn.loc.gov/2020050704

Editor: Jenna Gleisner
Designer: Molly Ballanger

Photo Credits: Vladimir Zhoga/Shutterstock, cover; Zurijeta/Shutterstock, 1; Pixfiction/Shutterstock, 3; Philip Lange/Shutterstock, 4, 8, 12-13; Jinu Philip Mathew/Shutterstock, 5; Universal Images Group/SuperStock, 6-7; trabantos/Shutterstock, 9; REUTERS/Alamy, 10-11; Michael Jenner/Alamy, 14-15; Stanislav71/Shutterstock, 16; Olha Solodenko/Shutterstock, 17; John Engel/Alamy, 18-19; Giuseppemasci/Dreamstime, 20-21; tanukiphoto/iStock, 23.

Printed in the United States of America at Corporate Graphics in North Mankato, Minnesota.

TABLE OF CONTENTS

CHAPTER 1

COUNTRY OF ISLANDS

Welcome to Bahrain! This country is in the Middle East. Temperatures can top 100 degrees Fahrenheit (38 degrees Celsius). The Tree of Life is here. It is more than 400 years old. How does it get water in a desert? No one knows!

Tree of Life

Manama is the **capital**. It is Bahrain's largest city, too. Almost half of the **population** lives here. The Bahrain World Trade Center is here. It stands 787 feet (240 meters) tall.

Bahrain World Trade Center

Bahrain is in the Persian Gulf. It is an **archipelago**. More than 30 islands make up this country.

The King Fahd Causeway is a string of bridges. It links Bahrain to Saudi Arabia. The causeway is 15 miles (24 kilometers) long. It is a fast way to cross the Persian Gulf!

Saudi Arabia

DID YOU KNOW?

Bahrain means "two seas" in Arabic. Why does it have this name? Freshwater **springs** are under the saltwater ocean that surrounds Bahrain.

Persian Gulf

Bahrain

King Fahd Causeway

CHAPTER 2
LIFE IN BAHRAIN

People first lived in this area in 2200 BCE. The Bahrain Fort is **ancient**. It was once an important trading center. Later, it became a **military** fort.

Bahrain Fort

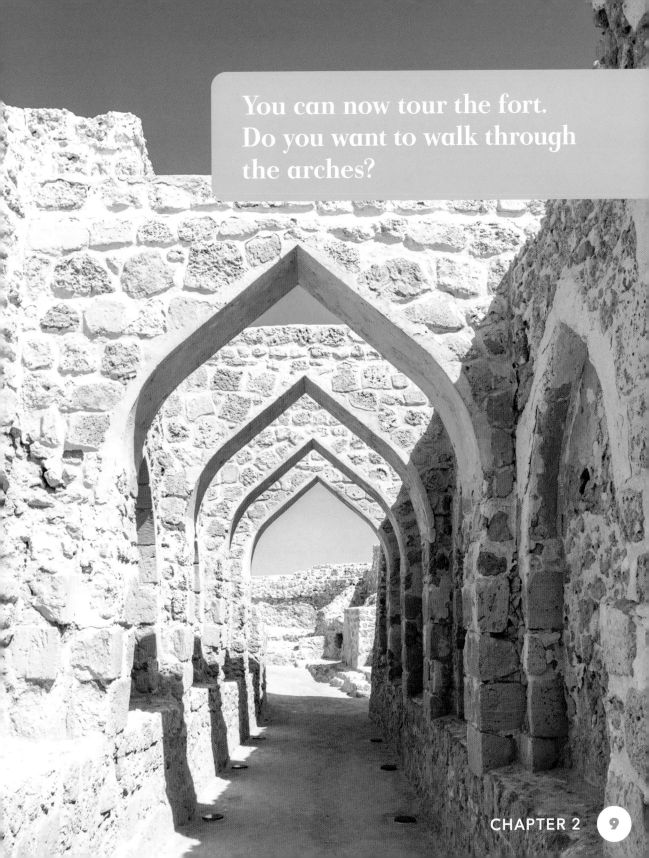

You can now tour the fort. Do you want to walk through the arches?

voting
ballot

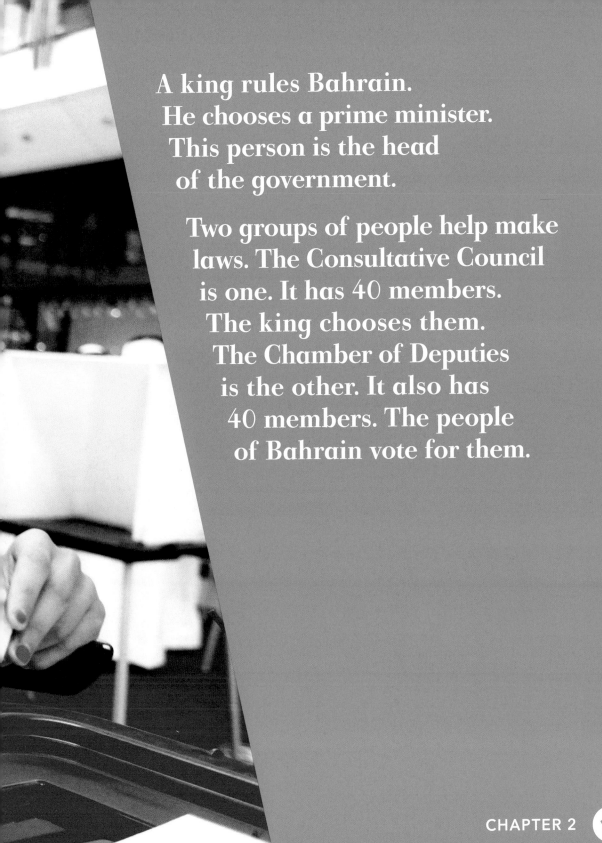

A king rules Bahrain. He chooses a prime minister. This person is the head of the government.

Two groups of people help make laws. The Consultative Council is one. It has 40 members. The king chooses them. The Chamber of Deputies is the other. It also has 40 members. The people of Bahrain vote for them.

Many people here pray in **mosques**. The Al Fateh Mosque is one of the largest in the world. It holds 7,000 people!

Al Fateh Mosque

TAKE A LOOK!

Many people here are **Muslim**. How does that compare to other religions? Take a look!

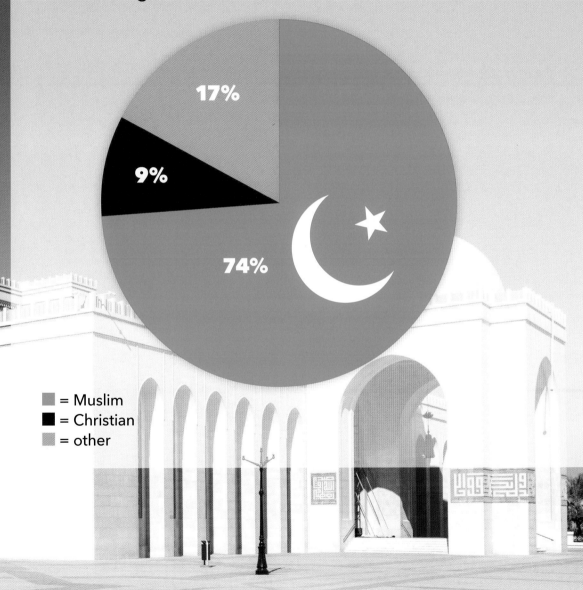

17%

9%

74%

■ = Muslim
■ = Christian
■ = other

Children go to school from age six to 14. They must pass a test to go longer. School is taught in Arabic. Students learn English, too. They wear uniforms.

WHAT DO YOU THINK?

Girls and boys go to separate public schools. Private schools have both boys and girls. Which would you prefer? Why?

CHAPTER 3

FOOD AND FUN

People share food dishes. They eat with their hands. Machboos is meat or fish made with spices. It is served with rice.

chicken machboos

dates

Dates are a popular treat. More than 500,000 date palm trees grow here.

Markets here are called souks. You can buy spices and sweets. You will also find fabrics, jewelry, and **traditional** clothing. You can **haggle** for a lower price!

WHAT DO YOU THINK?

How does your family shop? Do you go to stores? Do you order online? Would you like to shop at a souk?

spices

Would you like to ride an Arabian horse? There are more than 20 types here! People love to watch horse races. Camel racing is also popular.

Bahrain is an exciting country! Would you like to visit?

QUICK FACTS & TOOLS

BAHRAIN

Location: Middle East

Size: 301 square miles
(780 square kilometers)

Population: 1,505,003
(July 2020 estimate)

Capital: Manama

Type of Government:
constitutional monarchy

Languages: Arabic, English,
Farsi, Urdu

Exports: petroleum and petroleum
products, aluminum, textiles

Currency: Bahraini dinar

GLOSSARY

ancient: Belonging to a period long ago.

archipelago: A group of islands.

capital: A city where government leaders meet.

haggle: To work together to agree on the price of something.

military: Of or having to do with soldiers, the armed forces, or war.

mosques: Buildings where Muslims worship.

Muslim: People whose religion is Islam.

population: The total number of people who live in a place.

springs: Places where water rises to the surface from underground sources.

traditional: Having to do with the customs, beliefs, or activities that are handed down from one generation to the next.

Bahrain's currency

INDEX

TO LEARN MORE

Finding more information is as easy as 1, 2, 3.

❶ Go to www.factsurfer.com

❷ Enter "Bahrain" into the search box.

❸ Choose your book to see a list of websites.

FACT
SURFER

ALL AROUND THE WORLD

Every country has an interesting history as well as unique places to visit. Learn more about how people live all around the world in these fun and fact-filled books. Have you read them all?

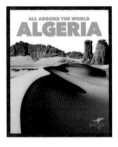
ALL AROUND THE WORLD
ALGERIA

ALL AROUND THE WORLD
AUSTRIA

ALL AROUND THE WORLD
BAHRAIN

ALL AROUND THE WORLD
FINLAND

ALL AROUND THE WORLD
HUNGARY

ALL AROUND THE WORLD
JAMAICA

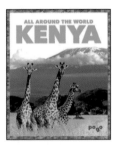
ALL AROUND THE WORLD
KENYA

ALL AROUND THE WORLD
KUWAIT

ALL AROUND THE WORLD
LAOS

ALL AROUND THE WORLD
MADAGASCAR

ALL AROUND THE WORLD
NEW ZEALAND

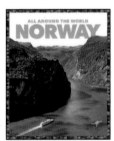
ALL AROUND THE WORLD
NORWAY

ALL AROUND THE WORLD
PANAMA

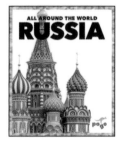
ALL AROUND THE WORLD
RUSSIA

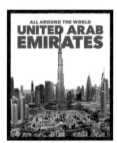
ALL AROUND THE WORLD
UNITED ARAB EMIRATES

IL: Grades 2–5   ATOS: 2.9

ju mp!

www.jumplibrary.com
www.jumplibrary.com/teachers

ISBN 978-1-64527-998-3

90000

9 781645 279983

SUPERFAST ROCKETS